Zac

Endogo book 7

Published by Crossbridge Books
Worcester
© Crossbridge Books 2025

ISBN 978-1-916945-16-6

British Library Cataloguing Publication Data. A catalogue record for this book is available from the British Library.

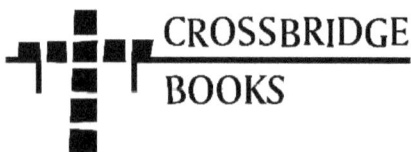

CROSSBRIDGE
BOOKS

Zac

Endogo book 7

by R M Price-Mohr

Vocabulary for book 7:

asleep
baby
been
before
blue
cannot
finding
flowers
follows
house
leaves
lost
make
more
mouse
needs
off
take/takes
them
Zac

Foreword for teachers

These books have been developed for older beginner readers. The research-based approach focuses on the recognition of just 100 key words that together make up approximately two-thirds of all reading matter in English. By the time the reader has learnt to recognise all the words in book 6, they will know 36 words that make up 33% of all reading matter in English written narrative.

For each new book, twenty new words are introduced and listed at the beginning of each book The new vocabulary for each book should be introduced to the learner in such a way that they will be able to recognise them at sight <u>before</u> reading the book. It is recommended that this is achieved through playing with the printed words. In the first instance, this should be by having two sets of printed and separated words in large font (minimum 20 point) that the beginner reader can match. It is crucial that the teacher continuously verbalise the words, and they may point to significant features in words, firstly the initial letters and secondly to any other distinctive features, to assist with the matching. Following this, the word recognition can be reinforced in games such as bingo, dominoes, snap, Pelmanism etc.

Some temptations to continue to avoid:

- Do not ask the reader to sound out all the individual letters of a word – only the initial letter has value at this stage for reading.
- Do not test the reader to see if they can recognise any of the words by telling you what they say – this should become obvious during the games; remember that visual recognition is not the same thing as verbalising what is seen.

This is Zac the endogo.

Zac has been finding some small twigs.

He needs to find some more to make a little house for a baby mouse.

The baby mouse cannot find its mother. It is lost.

The baby mouse is asleep next to the tall tree.

Lem wants to help make the little house.

"There are some more twigs by the blue flowers," said Zac.

Kat is by the blue flowers. She takes the leaves off the twigs.

"Can I help?" said Lem.

"We need to take the leaves off first before we take them to Zac," said Kat.

Kat and Lem take the leaves off.

The mother mouse is looking for her baby.

The mother mouse follows Kat and Lem.

The baby mouse follows his mother home.

High Frequency Words:

baby
been
before
blue
house
make
more
take
them

Word patterns:

_ake	make	_ee_	see
	take		seen
_ing	looking		green
	eating		tree
	going		keep
	climbing		needs
	having		asleep
_ouse	house	_st	lost
	mouse		fast
			first
			forest